Captivated

Who is this Man?

Captivated: Who is this Man?
By Ann Lindholm

Published by HIS Publishing House
Aurora, MO 65605

Email: info@authorannlindholm.com
https://www.hispublishinghouse.com

Copyright © 2021 by HIS Publishing House
All rights reserved.
ISBN: 978-0-578-96569-7

Scripture quotations are from The ESV® Bible (The Holy Bible, English Standard Version®), copyright© 2001 by Crossway Bibles, a publishing ministry of Good News Publishers. Used by permission. All rights reserved®.

All rights reserved. No part of this publication may be reproduced, stored in a retrieval system, or transmitted in any form or by any means—electronic, mechanical, photocopy, recording, or any other—except for brief quotations in printed reviews, without the permission of the Author or Publisher.

The digital format of Captivated, along with other titles can be purchased at: www.hispublishinghouse.com

Endorsements

So many believers spend the majority of their lives trying to please God, work harder for him and live in the constant fear that they aren't doing enough for him. This kind of thinking and living ends up crushing you. The truth is that our God is a Bridegroom and he has made us for himself. He has designed us for deep intimacy with him, knowing and encountering his affections for us and out of the overflow of that encounter, living a life with him. The Holy Spirit is calling his people to this reality in these days. He is doing this by anointing his friends to write, speak, and communicate these realities to people all over the world. I am so excited for the release of Ann Lindholm's new book called, "Captivated?" Ann opens her heart and through her own musings, thoughts, and writing, invites us into deep intimacy with God. I absolutely love this book and am so excited it's being released for such a time as this.—Corey Russell, Author of *Teach us to Pray* www.coreyrussellonline.com

In this hustle-bustle world, we rush from one obligation to the next at breakneck speed, leaving us feeling like time with the Lord is just one more item to check off. Author Ann Lindholm shows us another way, beckoning us to quit running and be still in His presence, the Lover of our soul. Through Lindholm's musings and meditations, we experience her captivation with her Savior and deepen our own intimacy with the One who created us. Grab a cup of coffee/tea, curl up with *Captivated*, and draw near to His throne of grace. He's already there waiting for you.—Candace Kirkpatrick, Actress www.candacekirkpatrick.com

The love of our Dad, the correction of our Father and the direction of our King, all wrapped up in the surrender of our hearts to Him…such are found in these pages. Read, ponder, rejoice and be as He is.—Camy "Cameron" Arnett, Camy Arnett Production Studios, www.savingdestinies.com

Contents

Foreword	6
Introduction	7
Musings	8
Dreams and Thoughts From the Lord	68
Acknowledgements	88
Reviews of Captivated	90
Titles by Ann Lindholm	92
About the Author	99

This book is dedicated to my Lover, my Groom, my King…his name is Jesus!

You have changed my life, my heart and my soul forever.
I long for the day when I can physically be in your arms
and feel the breath of your whisper in my ear.
I am preparing for you everyday.
I pray you find me ready.

Foreword

The world is full of junk food theology consumed in bits and pieces like a smorgasbord. Many students of God's word are surfers, riding the surface of living water seeking entertainment, self-help, or somewhere to excuse God's love and God's justice.

This book is a rare opportunity to experience the pain of love when someone becomes vulnerable to express the distress of personal experiences.

This author has explored and charted the spiritual and emotional depths herself, and you can almost hear the Shulamite woman in the Song of Solomon crying out to the King, "*She*-Let him kiss me with the kisses of his mouth! For your love is better than wine;" Song of Solomon 1:2 (ESV)

In this book, Ann Lindholm is not sharing shallow teachings for those who suffer from short attention spans, or those who refuse to be provoked to spiritual transformation. *Captivated; Who Is This Man* guides the reader through the Bible, painting beautiful word pictures that challenge us to face God's truth over worldly opinion. She addresses issues such as faith versus fear, and is the church "a culture" with moral influence, or has it become a powerless sub-culture that is out of sight and out of mind?

Ann connects God's words, heart, and promises with his expectations and judgments. This book elevates the reader's understanding of our daily decisions to be either victim of our circumstances or a servant to our Lord.

In reading this book, one can see that Ann Lindholm is passionate about the redeemed in Christ and the finished work of our Lord Jesus Christ in each of us. Her heart cries to see the body of Christ purified on the inside while manifesting a visible testimony on the outside for the world to behold.

Every man and woman born again is unique, and God's Spirit and God's Word is transforming them into a New Creation in Christ. God's gift of grace in giving up his Son to die for humanity offers us the fantastic opportunity to explore the depths of God's Word and God's love. See the author's vision of what believers can expect in the days to come as we become CAPTIVATED. Who is this man? Take a deep breath, immerse yourself in the Lord Jesus and His promise of living water, and go deeper.

Charles Morris
Author, Founder and CEO of RSIM, RSIP, and RSISoM

Introduction

Choose a comfy spot, recline, relax your heart and mind and allow Holy Spirit to minister to you in a very personal and fresh way. Lay aside all preconceived ideas of who God is. Seek to know him personally, deeply, intimately. Let him touch your heart. Seek with hunger and desire to know him and his character.

Allow the *Musings*, which are full of whispers the Lord has given me to marinate in your mind and let the Father minister to your heart. Through the years of my spiritual walk I have grown in many different ways. These last few years have been the most personal and intimate growth I have ever experienced. He has penetrated my soul, creating in me an insatiable yearning for more of him. I pray you will experience the same desire as you partake in the most amazing love story ever.

Also included in this book are dreams, visions and words that I believe the Lord shared with me. The main point in sharing these dreams are two-fold—I want to encourage you to be more attentive to how the Lord may speak to you and seek to learn more about what he is saying to you personally as well as to the Church; whether it be through dreams, visions or spoken words by others. Secondly, many of these dreams I believe pertain to all of the body of Christ. I believe he has spoken a message for us to not only hear but to respond to. I invite you into a keen awareness of his whispers all around. He desires to speak to you and he longs for you to speak to him.

May you be richly blessed as you read and listen for the voice of the Father. He loves you deeply and longs to have relationship with you. He desires to spend time with you one on one. Will you join me on this intimate journey as we purchase oil for our lamps from the Bridegroom (Matthew 25)?

Maranatha!

Musings

Captivated

There I lay, on my bed, a young girl about ten years old. I pored over the words he wrote in one of his love letters. Found in the scriptures and written for me, these letters changed my life. I was able to comprehend much of it, but parts were beyond my capacity to understand at such a young age. Oh, how I desired to know the meaning of every weighted word. I knew deep within my heart that every single word was special and just for me. His love letters inspired my dreams and visions I had throughout the night and day.

He would use these dreams and visions to captivate my heart even further for him. The earliest dream I recall started off with me as a young girl, a child, splashing about in my pop-up swimming pool on the lawn, so lush and green, like velvet. Warm sun rays kissed my golden skin. Children's laughter and play could be heard faintly in the background along with sounds of lawn mowers sending aromas of freshly cut lawns floating in the air. Cornstarch blue skies decorated the backdrop of this beautiful dream. And there he was, descending on a bright cloud, adorned in brilliant white linen with a golden sash draped around his chest. His hair, dark, wavy and past his neck. Eyes…oh his eyes were like fire! A smile beamed across his face, so warm and full of love. As he approached, his arms were out, palms up. Without even speaking he said so much to my young heart. I was truly captivated.
End of dream.

My windows are often open so I can feel the wind dancing through the curtains. It is as if I can hear his voice riding on every breeze. He is here. I can feel him. Without saying a word, he is here, with me. I am never alone. Birds are chirping and singing his love song. He loves me. I feel it. I feel him. Can you feel him? Can you hear his voice?

When I doubted and wondered if he was even real, he never abandoned me. I could always hear his voice and feel his presence. Even when I wasn't reciprocating his love, he never quit on me. All those years I was silent and wouldn't respond to his calls, he stayed, waiting for me. The only time he felt far off was when I wanted him to. He is such a gentleman. He has always been watching over me even when I didn't know or didn't want to believe it, there he was. I made some of the most painful decisions that carried the capacity to cut right to his heart. Yet, he was never offended. He keeps loving me. He keeps calling for me. He never gives up on me. Through all the times I rejected him, he stayed, waiting, like a jealous lover. He isn't going anywhere. He has all the time in the world. He holds time in his hands. He is patient. He…is love.

When I feel lonely, he is always available. I don't have to wait for him to complete a task or end a conversation with someone else. He is always captivated by me and desires for me to be in his presence. He never turns me away. He drops everything to hear my voice. He longs to hold me for hours on end. There is nothing more important or lovely to him than to hold me and call me his love. He strokes my hair like a loving father, cherishing every strand and every second of time with me. He stares into my eyes and sketches into his memory every single crease and sparkle, like a mother not wanting to forget this moment in time. He grabs a bundle of my hair drenched with the smell of the outdoors and draws it to his nostrils, sniffing a memory that will never fade. He is content to sit here, in this moment with me, not being distracted by anything else. Yet, his word holds the planets and constellations in place, but somehow, he is able to devote every iota of attention on me. I feel so treasured and loved. There is no rejection for me in his heart. He will stop everything for me. He will lay down his very life..for me…and yet, I cannot fathom what I have done to gain such love from this beautiful man. How have I captivated a king? How have I captivated THE King?

My mind cannot comprehend his love for me. My heart cannot fathom it. My emotions overflow with joy at his love for me. No man has loved me like this. No man has gone to such great length to win my heart. Yes, he has opened his store houses to me, but that is not what draws me. His desire for me, his love for me…oh his love. His presence. His presence awakens my soul. He causes me to want to dance and sing! He fills my heart with joyful laughter and cries of overwhelming gratitude. When I call out to him, his beaming smile saturates me with drunkenness for his love. I want more of him. Every encounter draws me to seek him further. I find myself searching and planning for ways to escape with him into a secluded place where we can get lost in each other. He is my lover! He is the man in that dream. He is the One I have been searching for since I was a little girl. I am my beloved's.

I found him, whom my soul loves.

Song of Solomon 3:4

Morning Awakening

Every morning my Bridegroom awakens me with birds singing his love song to me. An amazingly bright and enormous star peeks over the horizon, gently stirring me from my sleep. I make my way to the window and tell him good morning, thanking him for all the glorious beauty surrounding me. He knows my love language and speaks it to me constantly. Always prodding the depths of my heart with intimate knowledge of who I am, reminding me, I am forever his. I remain captivated by his love and longing for me. He is the lover of my soul!

Romans 1:20

Marriage Union

No greater intimacy, no greater love affair exists than that of the marriage union. Little girls dream of this day from their childhood. Boys imagine themselves as a warrior, fighting for their lady. Making wedding plans more extravagant than any party we've ever attended takes up residence in our mind and heart as we become young ladies. We didn't arrive at this day all at once. It began with a wink, or a gentle smile that spoke a thousand words. It began before that with our desire to be loved, cherished, valued, honored and wanted. I've searched from my childhood for that man who could love me so deeply, so perfectly. I longed for a handsome man who would forever protect me and fight for me. I wanted someone to laugh with. I dreamed of a man who would play with me, run with me, picnic with me and romance me.

This man showed glimpses of himself to me. He seemed distant, untouchable, unreal. Yet, my heart longed to believe in him and my mind desired to bring him into reality. He would show up in the oddest of places. At times I wasn't even thinking about him, he would appear in my dreams, a place where fantasy and reality collide. He revealed himself to me in ways that I will carry forever.

At times he would speak to me through a friend or a teacher. He would hold my hand through a classmate's hand during morning prayer. I might catch a glimpse of his face in the clouds or hear his whisper in the wind. Although I wasn't searching for him, he showed up. For many years he hung out in the background. He invited me to youth group nights through friends. Through close girlfriends he would speak truth to my heart. His beautiful face would show up in posters hanging in the mall, or on the front cover of a book. This man was everywhere.

When I was making bad decisions, he was somehow there, speaking to my heart, saying, "You are worth more than this. You are valuable. I would never treat you this way. I love you. I love you even now, in the midst of your behavior, I love you. Please, come to me. I have so much more for you than this." He would cause these feelings in my gut to rumble, making me realize that what I was doing wasn't right, yet, his love was all around me. He wasn't ashamed of me. He wasn't angry with me. When I ran away, he ran with me. He watched over me in miraculous ways, protecting me. Bad choice after bad choice, he still wanted me to be his.

My lover fought for me relentlessly. He chased after me. He pursued me. He fought off my enemies. He wooed me. He saw my worth despite my inability to see it. He saw beyond my selfish choices and mistakes. Having full knowledge of the worst mistake that I could ever make, he loved me and called me to be his prize. He pierced through to my heart. He took all that I messed up and repaired it. He took his own blood and washed away my guilt. He stood in my place in the court of judgment, defending my case. He paid my ransom. He presented me to the Judge as pardoned, freed, liberated, spotless, pure and holy.

And then, he took me on a journey of amazing love and intimacy. It is the greatest love story ever told. We began spending time together. He would speak to me through the most holy book. He invited me into his heart, into his throne room. Much of what he said drew me in, seeking for more. Who was this man that he knew everything about me? Who was this man that he saw beyond my imperfections and still loved me? This man is Jesus, Yeshua.

John 3:16; John 15:13; Song of Solomon 2:10

Beauty

Although thorns are present along the stem, her strength is deeply rooted in the soil. Her stem supplies water and nutrients that feed sturdy leaves and amazing petals of vibrant color. With every turn of the hour her petals open wide, producing a robust bloom full of beauty and vibrance. Her fragrance is tantalizing, going following you all day long.

Jesus supplies a strong foundation deeply rooted in his word and in spite of our thorny past, he works in and through us, birthing beauty that pleases those around us. The fragrance of our testimony stays with those who hear it. His presence is ever increasing in us, just as the bloom continually opens and grows. Not much needs to be said if we are exposing his beauty.

2 Corinthians 2:14-15

Our citizenship is not of this world.

We belong to the Kingdom of God!

This Life

When I consider the blessings of my birth in a free nation I am stumped by how life works and how it is that I am here and not there. Why was I born in the United States of America? Is that significant and if so, why? Do I consider my birthplace a gift from God? Is it about where I live, or is it more about "how" I live?

The nations and the lands belong to God, not man. He can tear down just as quickly as he created. I must believe that it is more about how I live rather than where I live. It has to be more about my heart condition toward Jesus and others. If I fully believe that the Bible is true and that God is who he says he is, then I must also believe that eternity is real. There is a life beyond this physical body and how I live and what I believe should dictate my life now in order to affect my life for eternity. I must learn to love like Jesus, to see like Jesus. I must go lower and elevate him higher. I must become a servant as he became a servant. What does that even look like?

Lord, please help me to genuinely desire to understand and know others. Please help me to have a heart for the lost, the hurting, and the forgotten. Show me how to love like you love. I want to feel for others what you feel. Help me to lay my desires and selfishness down, and truly lift others up. Help me think before I speak. "How will this affect the heart of those who will hear what I say?" Father, I desire that all those around me would encounter Jesus when they encounter me. I lay my life down, that includes my preferences and desires. I need your help Lord, to love like you love. Amen.

Matthew 5-7; Romans 15; Galatians and Ephesians 5; John 15:13

JESUS is literally the ONLY Answer!

In The Night

I cannot count the ways my Love speaks to me. My restless mind recycles the events of the day like a hamster on a wheel. My eyes won't stay shut and my body is too active for sleep. Then, he steps in and sends a gentle rain that plays melodies on my rooftop.

Gentle breezes saunter through the open windows and wisp over my cheeks and through my hair. I can hear the dripping of the rain sliding off the house onto the concrete patio. Soft rolls of thunder begin to play a rhythm that causes my mind to slow down. Refreshing. Washing. Lullaby of the night.

The rain speeds up and intensifies as lightning joins the chorus. He reminds me of his power and his majesty. He is telling me he is in control and he is on my side. He whispers in my ear that he is bigger than I know. He is telling my enemies that I am his and he is mine. He is reminding my foes that his eyes watch over me. "Rest easy my love, I've got you." The intensity of the storm slows and trickles of rain soften the mood. Bullfrogs begin to croak and crickets chirp. A few nocturnal birds sing a song as the owl watches in the night. All is well.

He is with me. I can rest easy. A tawny moon peaks through rain clouds, lighting the night and waiting to welcome the morning sun.

Song of Solomon 6:3; Psalm 29:1; Jeremiah 10:13-15

Walking on Water

Reclining on the rocks of the lakeshore, my gaze fixes upon the water as I daydream about that stormy night when Jesus approached the boat, walking on the water.

Did he intend for them to see him? Did he solidify the water to walk on it, or was he literally walking on liquid? Did they fully know who Jesus was and all that he was capable of? Would I have jumped out into the stormy water as Peter did, or would I have stayed securely in the boat, wishing I had the courage to jump into the water?

Lord, please help me to move forward in boldness and courage. Help me to radically pursue you as Peter did. I pray that I don't allow what others think of me to prevent me from chasing after you. Help me to pursue you more deeply Abba. Amen.

Matthew 14

Morning Conversations

How I long to meet with you in the early hours for our secret time, when no one else is awake. Your tender song awakens me with the morning glow of the sun. Birds singing, deer panting, humming birds hover over their nectar. Your words are waiting for me, to speak something special to awaken my heart. I'm listening Abba.

I see a tree in the distance shaped like a cross, with what looks like arms raising a "Hallelujah." Behind that cross shaped tree is the burning sun. You show me how glorious the message of the cross is. Your only Son gave his life for me upon that cross. Please, help me to never take it for granted. Help me to never lose sight of the gravity of the cross.

Thank you Jesus, for giving your life for me. Help me to live it the way you would. Help me to realize that you also died for my fellow man. As you gave your life for me, you also gave it for them. Help me to walk in love, grace and mercy. Amen.

John 3:16; John 15:13; Matthew 27; Mark 15; John 19

Be Still

"I long to sit with you in the still of the day, to be in your presence. My child, I love you. I adore you. Your smile brings my heart such pleasure. The sparkle in your eye brings my spirit great joy. How you wonder and seek to know. How you search. Your childlike faith saturates me with pleasure. Carefree. Not anxious. Restful. Always hungry. Hands-on. Trusting. Eager to obey. So giving and ready to share what you have with me. To hear you voice rise in song in adoration of me, oh my child how I love you! Your prayers, they are music to my ears, incense rising to heaven." — Love, your Father.

Revelation 8:4; Matthew 18

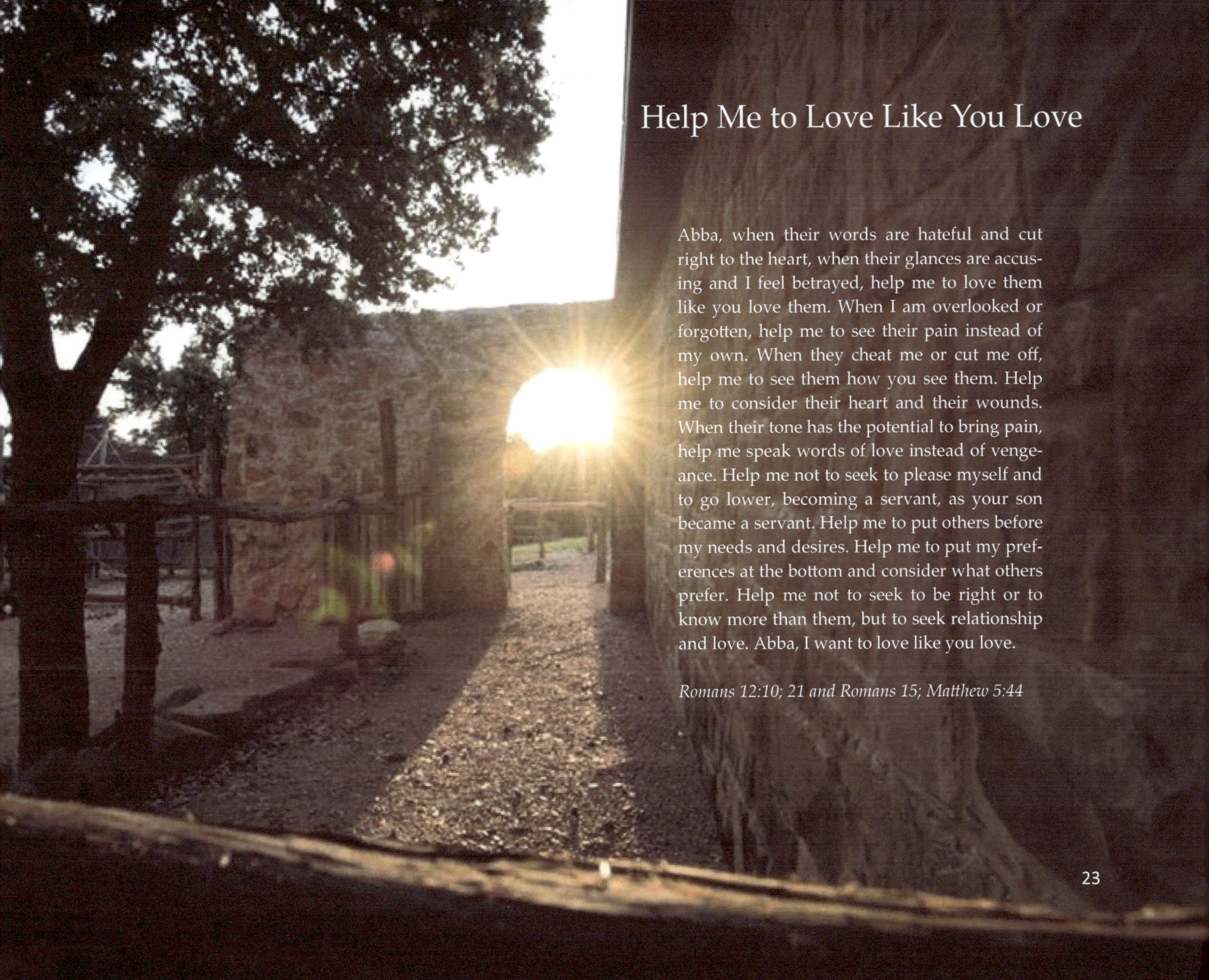

Help Me to Love Like You Love

Abba, when their words are hateful and cut right to the heart, when their glances are accusing and I feel betrayed, help me to love them like you love them. When I am overlooked or forgotten, help me to see their pain instead of my own. When they cheat me or cut me off, help me to see them how you see them. Help me to consider their heart and their wounds. When their tone has the potential to bring pain, help me speak words of love instead of vengeance. Help me not to seek to please myself and to go lower, becoming a servant, as your son became a servant. Help me to put others before my needs and desires. Help me to put my preferences at the bottom and consider what others prefer. Help me not to seek to be right or to know more than them, but to seek relationship and love. Abba, I want to love like you love.

Romans 12:10; 21 and Romans 15; Matthew 5:44

He Became a Servant

How is it that my King willingly stepped down from his heavenly throne and lowered himself to become a servant? He chose not to seek his own pleasure, rather to put other's before himself. A king? My King has knelt at the feet of sinners, taken the cloth from his waist, with water and washed their dirty, rugged, tired feet. The Beautiful One chose to accept persecution and ridicule on my behalf. Not once did he defend himself or fight back. Instead, he healed the ear of his enemy. His rightful place is positioned high upon the throne of the king of Kings. His rightful title is King of kings. His rightful inheritance is the Kingdom of Heaven. Yet, he chose to lower himself and become a servant.

My King, my Lord, please help me to purge all the pride, arrogance, and selfishness from my heart. I want to love the way you love. I want to know how to go lower. I want to know how to serve. I lay it all at your feet and surrender all that I have to you. Teach me to become a servant Lord. Amen.

Luke 22; John 13; Romans 15; Philippians 2

Blessing His Enemies

Bound with ropes, scourged beyond recognition, drenched in blood…he stood before his enemies and spoke not a word of defense. He was mocked and called demon-possessed. But he knew the truth. He knew who he was, what his position was and he knew who his father was. That is all that mattered. They spit in his face and attempted to give him wine mixed with gall. He hung nearly naked upon a cross along with two criminals as the Roman guards gambled his clothes away…and he prayed for them to be forgiven. They called him a blasphemer, yet he chose not defend himself. What kind of a man does this? What kind of a man stands silently in the face of persecution? He is the man! He is Jesus!

Matthew 27; Mark 15; John 19

Oh, the Soul of a Sinner!

It is for the soul of the wicked, the sinner, that we should be interceding. For we know the soul of a Believer will be reunited with Christ in total peace and full glory!

The soul of a sinner, oh the soul of a sinner...is damned to hell! True justice occurs through the cross, through a life laid down by a King, when sinners are saved from the clutches of sin, Satan and hell!

For the soul of the sinner he hung on that splintered cross, laying down his life even unto death. So shall our hearts bleed for the lost, longing to carry them with us into our King's eternal glory, forever and ever. Amen.

Matthew 27; Mark 15; John 19; 2 Corinthians 5; 2 Peter 3

The Heart of the Matter

The Lord is calling us into intimacy with him. He wrote an eternal love letter that gives us a blueprint for how he's calling us to enter into relationship with him. As we accept this invitation to dine on his Word and come into fellowship with him his Spirit reveals the glory of his Son. This unifies those who are pursuing him wholeheartedly. As believers seek to know Jesus through his Living Word a revival, a transformation of hearts begins to influence the environment. This is how we disciple. This is how we change a community.

As pastors and spiritual leaders meet in the Secret Place with the Bridegroom the overflow of those meetings seeps out into the congregation. The results of them communing with the Father in secret is made apparent as they preach, teach and lead. As Jesus is manifested among them. As the Living Word washes and purifies, as the fire of Jesus kindles their hearts the overflow pours out onto those around them. The love of Jesus is contagious.

To truly know God we accept his invitation to open his love letter, pondering every thought and word. We enter into dialogue with a Holy God. We dine at the table of the King. We recline at the campfire, leaning back into his chest, breathing in every breath of his. We study him. We ask him questions. Oh, how he loves to dialogue with us! How he longs for us to sit in his presence.

I used to believe a certain way on many political and social issues, but as I continually study the Word and discover God's character through intimate fellowship with him, I find that my thinking is often not in line with his. I discover that he's calling me to align with the culture of the kingdom of Heaven and in return, bring that culture into existence here on earth. Genuinely following God will not be popular and

will be hated by many, including many within in the Church. Ponder that for a moment. Are you ready? Yet, he is a magnificent God! He is worthy! He is worth everything we have. Corey Russell often quotes David in our Bible Study Zoom calls, "I don't want to bring a sacrifice that costs me nothing." (2 Samuel 24:14). Radically pursuing Jesus will cost us something, it will cost us everything…and it is worth it all beloved.

As we lay down our fleshly desires and chase after Jesus, we discover that literally nothing else matters. As we become spiritually minded the darkness gets pushed back. I pray that we not get blinded by the things of this earth and that we discover how to grow in the knowledge of God as we seek to behold him and become like him.

Father, we desire to know you more intimately. We desire to exalt you in all things, in every way. We desire to influence our community for your kingdom. Help us lay down anything that interrupts this. You are glorious, magnificent and highly exalted. We praise you Lord! Amen.

Romans 8 and 12; Ephesians 1 and 5; and Matthew 6:4

The Lord is Sifting a Generation

(Written on 03JUN2020 during COVID19 Pandemic and national civil unrest, protests and riots.)

The Lord began a major sifting in February 2020 when the entire world was put on lock-down. As we were drawn out of our public worship houses he was calling us into deep, intimate fellowship with him. He has been exposing lukewarmness and hypocrisy. He is calling us to realize that true intimacy with him begins in the privacy of our fellowship with him. He desires for us to partake in fervent prayer. He is calling us into an audience of One. He wants us to break through the awkwardness of solitary praise and worship. Abba is calling us into the love affair of a lifetime!

This has been a time of testing and sifting—do we really know this man Jesus? Are we seeking fellowship with Abba when no one is looking? Lord, we hear you calling us to you. We want to answer. We desire to answer the knock on the door of our hearts and allow you into every room of our being. We give you permission to search us oh God.

Lord prepare us for the intensifying heat and tribulations to come as we sit with you, studying you and being washed by you.

He has given us a strategy for how to prepare. He longs for a spotless Bride. He is showing us how to be purified and washed. Let us go now and buy oil from this Messiah.

The days are approaching where our total reliance on and surrender to God is what will sustain us. Will we endure until the end? Are we ready to truly follow Jesus, and lay our life down as he laid his down? Will we will be told, "Well done good and faithful servant."

Beloved, let us prepare our lamps and purchase our oil now. Come, let us go into the Secret Place, he is waiting for us! Maranatha!

Matthew 25; Revelation 1-3

What Others Think

If we're affected or shaken by what others think of us then we're seeking man's reward and not the Lord's.

A life devoted to Christ secretly will eventually be rewarded publicly.

Matthew 6:4; Galatians 1 and 1 Thessalonians 2

Lord Help us to Make Your Church Essential Again

God, open the eyes of your children. Lift the veil. Bring the revelation of Truth, the man Jesus. Awaken your soldiers! Lead us into repentance and healing. Help us carry the ministry of reconciliation to the nations. Give us a heart like yours Abba. Help us to love like you love. Help us to go lower. Show us how to become servants like your Son Jesus became a servant. Holy Spirit, teach us—teach us how to pray, teach us how to serve, teach us how to open our eyes and understand. Fill us with fire from heaven with compassion in our hearts. Abba, help us to make your House, your Church, essential again. In Jesus' name, amen!

Romans 15; 2 Corinthians 5; 2 Timothy 2:4

King Jesus!

I see you riding on the clouds on a beautiful white stallion built for war, rushing in with your armies pulling up the rear guard. The earth quakes and trembles in thunderous choirs as the horses stampede over the horizon, clouds of dust form billows of glory around you and your Army. The trumpets sound. The angels sing and shout your praises, "All hail King Jesus! Holy, Holy, Holy is the Lord! Great and mighty is he!" We lift our banners and our voices in unison as our King rides in victory as he's already conquered our enemy. You'll clothe us in fine white, linen robes and give us a new name; we fall to our knees, prostrate before your Majesty! You are glorious! You are magnificent! You are beautiful and awesome in every way. All the creatures of the earth sing your praises! The celebration of ALL time has begun! If David had reason to dance undignified, we have even more reason to dance relentless, unrestrained, unceasingly before our great and mighty Warrior, Prince of Peace! Unending worship. Unending heavenly bliss. Unending presence. All hail King Jesus! He is Lord, Lord of all. He is the Lamb, the Lion of Judah! He is the Prince of Peace! He is Redeemer! He is Holy! He is Judge! He is God Almighty! He is the Rose of Sharon! He is the Bread of Life! The Living Water! The New Wine! He is the Great I Am! HE IS!!!!

2 Samuel 6; Psalm 149 and 150 and Revelation

Daddy Loves You!

Abba loves you so much! No matter how massive your mistake or how deeply you've fallen, he loves you! He desires for you to return to him if you've walked away. If you haven't, he longs to spend more time with you! He thinks you're beautiful! His promises are faithful and true! There's nothing you can do to receive his forgiveness but to accept what his Son Jesus did for you on the cross. He offers abundant life free from bondage and sin! Say, "Yes!" to Jesus!

Love

The love we give and show isn't always reciprocated. It's at this point that love truly becomes a choice, an act of faith and, often...requires an act of the Holy Spirit. It's at this point that we realize it's not about us or our feelings or what we'll receive in return, rather it's about Jesus' command to love one another.

Love is something we must train in and practice continually.

Love isn't concerned about our feelings over theirs.
Love is not seeking revenge or retaliation.
Love responds tenderly to harshness.
Love seeks to edify in the midst of receiving criticism.
Love is fueled by prayer and strengthened by Holy Spirit.
Love defeats evil.
Love sees beyond the storm clouds.
Love NEVER gives up.

Love is patient, love is kind. It does not envy, it does not boast, it is not proud. It does not dishonor others, it is not self-seeking, it is not easily angered, it keeps no record of wrongs. Love does not delight in evil but rejoices with the truth. It always protects, always trusts, always hopes, always perseveres.
1 Corinthians 13:4-7

Matthew 22; 1 Corinthians 13; Philippians 2

Awake, Awake O' Sleeper!

Oh Church, awaken! Awake, awake O sleeper! Brothers, sisters...hear from the Lord. He is calling us to quit chasing after idols, false gods and worldly pleasures. Seek the Lord for he is good! Seek his knowledge! Seek to know him personally! Let us hear the Word of the Lord. Where there is no faithfulness of steadfast love, or no knowledge of God in the land, let us draw near to the God of Ebenezer, the God who assists us in our battle. Lord, we lay down the swearing, lying, murdering, stealing, adultery and bloodshed. We shed them of our mind, body and spirit. We lay them at the foot of your cross. We choose to lay them down and pickup our cross and follow you. Lord, we don't want to be destroyed for lack of knowledge. We desire knowledge, knowledge of you, knowledge of the Holy. We acknowledge our guilt and we seek your face Abba! We are seeking you God! We are returning to you oh Lord. You are our living hope, our ever-present help, our tower of refuge! We thank you Father, for healing our wounds and acquitting our transgressions. We thank you for washing us clean with the powerful, life-flowing blood of your Son, Jesus, the Slain Lamb. Hallelujah! We give you glory God of the nations, God of all creation.

"Hear the word of the Lord, O children of Israel, for the Lord has a controversy with the inhabitants of the land. There is no faithfulness or steadfast love, and no knowledge of God in the land; there is swearing, lying, murder, stealing, and committing adultery; they break all bounds, and bloodshed follows bloodshed." Hosea 4:1-2

"My people are destroyed for lack of knowledge; because you have rejected knowledge, I reject you from being a priest to me. And since you have forgotten the law of your God, I also will forget your children. The more they increased, the more they sinned against me; I will change their glory into shame. They feed on the sin of my people; they are greedy for their iniquity."
Hosea 4:6-8

"They shall eat, but not be satisfied; they shall play the whore, but not multiply, because they have forsaken the Lord to cherish whoredom, wine, and new wine, which take away the understanding. My people inquire of a piece of wood, and their walking staff gives them oracles. For a spirit of whoredom has led them astray, and they have left their God to play the whore." Hosea 4: 10-12

A wind has wrapped them in its wings, and they shall be ashamed because of their sacrifices."
Hosea 4:1:19

"I will return again to my place, until they acknowledge their guilt and seek my face, and in their distress earnestly seek me."
Hosea 5:15

But then…

"Come, let us return to the Lord; for he has torn us, that he may heal us; he has struck us down, and he will bind us up. After two days he will revive us; on the third day he will raise us up, that we may live before him. Let us know; let us press on to know the Lord; his going out is sure as the dawn; he will come to us as the showers, as the spring rains that water the earth."
Hosea 6:1-3

Let us know; let us press on to know the Lord!

Criticism is rooted in pride.
Pride comes from the pits of hell.

The more I surrender to Jesus,
the more I realize I need
to surrender to Jesus.

Biblical Division

The ONLY division that is righteous is:

Light vs. Dark (Principalities)
Good vs. Evil
Right vs. Wrong
Love vs. Hate
Humility vs. Pride
Generosity vs. Greed
Honor vs. Dishonor

Ephesians 5 and 1 Peter 2

The mariners asked Jonah,

"What is your occupation?"

"I fear the Lord, the God of heaven!"

Jonah 1

Prayer for Our Nation

28JUN2018

My Lord, Your Honor, Great Judge;

I come to you today, the 27th day of June in the year 2018, as an heir to your Kingdom by the blood of your Son, Jesus Christ of Nazareth, in humble confession of your people of the United States of America. I confess on her behalf all the ungodly acts that we have allowed in this nation through implementation of law and silence in the making thereof: The murder of unborn babies who should receive the greatest protection of all; the condoning of homosexual marriage and the forcing of churches to comply in conducting the ceremonies; the recognition and forced acceptance of transgenderism, tampering with your perfect will and creation; the entering into of treaties with ungodly nations; the protection of foreign religions and false gods and utter disregard for Christianity; the removing of your name and Law from public places; and the mishandling of funds and taxes toward ungodly activities. In solemn prayer I seek your forgiveness of these abominations and ask for your great grace and mercy. Above all, I ask that you burden your people of this nation with a love and desire for you and all things godly, just and right. Plant seeds of hunger, desire and yearning to know you personally and deeply. I ask that the ancient flood gates of revival be busted wide open and that your anointing be poured out upon this nation birthing the greatest revival in all of history. Bring your people to a great awakening in this nation my Lord.

May your presence fall heavily upon this land as never before seen or experienced. Birth a new excitement in your preachers, teachers and leaders. Hit Washington D.C. with your glory! Fall upon our governmental leaders with such an outpouring of your divine presence that revival breaks out on The Hill! Raise up our men to take their place of spiritual leadership in the home, churches and workplace. Show them how to lead with godly integrity and moral fortitude and strength. Raise our women to be godly, pure, modest wives, mothers and leaders of our children.

My Lord, we ask that you hear our prayers, help our land and lead us into spiritual victory for your glory and for your Kingdom!

Amen!   2 Chronicles 7 and Psalm 118

Victim vs. Servant

When we accept the title of victim it becomes easier to partner with manipulation of others. Manipulation is of the kingdom of darkness.

Let us rather, take on the title of servant of Christ and be liberated from what others think and what we *believe* others think of us. Let us respond instead, with genuine love and compassion for others, even if they misunderstand us.

No greater love…

John 8:36 and 15:13; Romans 6 and 15; Galatians 5 and 1 Peter 2

What Drives Us?

28JUN2020

Lord, we desire to be a living, walking testimony of your love to those around us. Let our lives be a fragrant offering to you as we minister love and reconciliation to those around us. Lord, while we enjoy political freedom let our hearts not rely on it. Let our hearts and spirit be prepared to come into agreement with the truth that the freedom you provide is the only freedom we desire, the only freedom that matters. For as long as we are living in the Spirit, we are free indeed!

I am truly free when I am willing to lose my life while sharing Jesus with an enemy. If I fight for my personal political freedom on earth but deny showing Jesus to the world, I am not truly free. Lord, you tell us, "No greater love has any man than if he lay down his life for his brother." (John 15:13) Father, bring this truth to life in our hearts. Help us to truly understand what this means and what it looks like to walk it out. We surrender ourselves to you. We lay down our personal rights and freedom; our preferences and choices, and seek to lay our lives down for our brothers and sisters. Amen.

Proverbs 2 and 22; John 2 and 10; *Romans 15; 1 Corinthians 10; 2 Corinthians 2 and 5* and Colossians 3

Abba is Speaking to My Heart

29JUN2020

I can only be obedient to what Abba is speaking to my heart. It doesn't always make sense or feel good in the flesh. I've been quite challenged spiritually to say the least, in the first six months of 2020. What he's been laying on my heart most likely is not a popular, feel-good message, but I know it's his heart.

We've made idols out of many things in our very comfortable America.

Revelation 1-3

A Far Greater Freedom

29JUN2020

Father is looking for repentant hearts. My husband is a US Army Ranger and he's been in battles which video games can never compete. He's lost too many comrades on the battlefield. My family has sacrificed not only in the nine years he served and the four he contracted, but the effects of war still hang out in the hallways of his mind. So, I understand freedom. I understand the cost of political freedom. It is good to promote political freedom, equality and justice. There are times where God may call us to engage in physical battles to defend political freedom, but we must heed the Father's voice and be led by his Spirit.

What my relationship with the Lord has revealed to me is that there is a freedom far greater and way beyond political freedom. That freedom only exists in relationship with Jesus Christ. That freedom should be defended and promoted above all other freedoms. When we promote political freedom above Kingdom of God freedom we've begun serving a different god.

Lord help us have an eternal mindset. Lord, we want to serve you and you alone. We accept the freedom that the blood of your Son, Jesus, bought for us. We recognize it is enough; it is sufficient. We give you glory for this freedom.

This earth as we know it will pass away. America, as great a nation as she is, is not our savior. America will cease to exist one day…Lord, help us comprehend this reality. Help us step away from shortsightedness and truly begin walking and living with an eternal mindset. Help us recognize your true authority and kingship. Lord, I pray that we are attentive to your voice and obedient to your calling to follow the Shepherd. Help us not rely on earthly things but to see you as our only Provider. Help us live by the Spirit. Amen

These are the days! Maranatha!

John 8; Romans 9; Philippians 4

The Full Gospel

Lord, help us not to taint your message of grace, mercy and justice. Help us understand what true justice is and that it costs you everything.

In studying Jeremiah, Amos, Joel, Zephaniah, Habakkuk, Hosea, Nahum, Micah, Jonah, Isaiah...all should cause every believer to awaken their heart to the crisis we are in. Add to this Revelation 18.

Though God has used Babylon (at that time recognized by all as the greatest world power) to bring judgment on other nations, he despised their intense pride and arrogance when they lived as they pleased while scorning the laws and standards of God's Word. God's Word makes it clear that what happened to ancient Babylon (present day Iraq), will happen to all ungodly people and nations in the last days.

Friends, this should cause us to tremble. Those who are prophesying only peace and grace are not prophesying for the Lord! The Lord prophesies to bring us into reconciliation with him. This usually calls for an adjustment in our hearts, a laying down of our lives and picking up our cross. He is the only fountain worthy of drinking from. Let us go to him, all who are weary. Let us run to him, our tower of refuge. Let us call on him, our ever-loving Father, so full of grace and mercy.

Look at what we've done as a nation since our inception (I'm sure more can be added):

- Remove God from schools, court houses, legislative body, public squares and even many churches.
- Not only allowed but enforced homosexual marriage, abortion, and sex-trafficking (a prettier word for slavery).
- Raised up idols and images above God.
- Become reliant on self-preservation and independence.
- Become extremely greedy
- Become lazy as a people.

- Elevated man, sports figures, political leaders, political party above God.
- Elevated television and Hollywood above God.
- Allowed the destruction of God-ordained and designed family structure.
- Allowed, endorsed and practiced extreme sexual immorality.
- Allowed and endorsed racial preference/prejudice within our society.
- Proudly defied and opposed the Lord.
- Given in to hatred, animosity and anger towards our brothers and sisters.
- Holding on to unforgiveness.
- Lacking repentant attitudes
- Neglected the studying and teaching of God's Word and replaced it with a hyper-grace, prosperity message, neglecting the full Gospel message that includes the death, resurrection and return of a Bridegroom for a prepared and ready Bride.
- Revelation 18:1-3 (You'll want to read this!)
- Revelation 18:9–"Kings (leaders) of the earth have committed sexual immorality and lived in luxury..." (Sound familiar?)

Friends, the Lord is calling us to, "Come out of her my people, lest you take part in her sins, lest you share in her plagues; for her sins are heaped high as heaven, and God has remembered her iniquities." (Rev 18:4-5)

God's kindness is meant to lead us to repentance. (Romans 2:4) We are to see his slowness to anger and judgment as a gracious, merciful and kind opportunity to walk in repentance and seek his face, turning from our sinful ways!

Now is the time!
Seize the day!

SEEK THE LORD!
For he is good!

"Who shall ascend the hill of the Lord? And who shall stand in his holy place?

He who has clean hands and a pure heart, who does not lift up his soul to what is false and does not swear deceitfully.

He will receive blessing from the Lord and righteousness from the God of his salvation.

Such is the generation of those who seek him, who seek the face of the God of Jacob.

Lift up your heads, O gates!
And be lifted up, O ancient doors,
that the King of glory may come in.
Who is the King of glory?
The Lord, strong and mighty,
the Lord, mighty in battle!
Lift up your heads, O gates!
And lift them up, O ancient doors,
that the King of glory may come in.
Who is the King of glory?

THE LORD OF HOSTS,
HE IS THE KING OF GLORY!"

Psalm 24:3-10

Until we truly have a heart for the lost, we have yet to personally encounter the man Jesus.

Matthew 9:35-38; Luke 19:10; 2 Peter 3:9 and 1 Corinthians 9

Unwavering Faith

- He did not weaken in faith when he considered the circumstances!
- No unbelief made him waver concerning the promise of God!
- He grew strong in his faith *as* he gave glory to God!
- Fully convinced that God was able to do what he had promised!

Romans 4:13-25

For the promise to Abraham and his offspring that he would be heir of the world did not come through the law but through the righteousness of faith. For if it is the adherents of the law who are to be the heirs, faith is null and the promise is void. For the law brings wrath, but where there is no law there is no transgression.

That is why it depends on faith, in order that the promise may rest on grace and be guaranteed to all his offspring—not only to the adherent of the law but also to the one who shares the faith of Abraham, who is the father of us all, as it is written, "I have made you the father of many nations"—in the presence of the God in whom he believed, who gives life to the dead and calls into existence the things that do not exist. In hope he believed against hope, that he should become the father of many nations, as he had been told, "So shall your offspring be." He did not weaken in faith when he considered his own body, which was as good as dead (since he was about a hundred years old), or when he considered the barrenness of Sarah's womb. No unbelief made him waver concerning the promise of God, but he grew strong in his faith as he gave glory to God, fully convinced that God was able to do what he had promised. That is why his faith was "counted to him as righteousness." But the words "it was counted to him" were not written for his sake alone, but for ours also. It will be counted to us who believe in him who raised from the dead Jesus our Lord, who was delivered up for our trespasses and raised for our justification.

Expressions

Our facial expressions, body language and tone of voice reveal a whole lot more about what's in our heart than our words could ever express.

Oh Lord, please cleanse my heart. Lord, transform me to have a heart like yours because I definitely can't do it in my own strength. Amen.

Genesis 4:6; Isaiah 3:9; Proverbs 4:23

Every Good Work

Oh Lord, please help me to follow your lead, to do your will and to hear your voice. Holy Spirit, please help me walk in gentleness and love. Help me to walk in submission and obedience to authorities and rulers as you have called your people to do. Help me to recognize and avoid foolish controversies, dissensions and quarrels. Help me not to stir up dissension. Please forgive me for the times that I participated in such things. Help me to show perfect courtesy toward all people. Thank You for the washing, regeneration and renewal of the Holy Spirit. Amen!

Titus 3:1-9

Honoring Those in Leadership

I've always found it interesting that Paul recognized he was wrong in speaking disrespectfully to a man who held a position of leadership. Now, these were religious leaders who also held positions of legal/governmental standing in their community. The fact that Paul recognized the requirement and need to honor those in authority is amazing.

I haven't always done this. What if I was in a similar situation? Would I be willing to admit I was wrong and apologize for dishonoring the one who's leading a legal case and physical harm against me?

And looking intently at the council, Paul said, "Brothers, I have lived my life before God in all good conscience up to this day." And the high priest Ananias commanded those who stood by him to strike him on the mouth. Then Paul said to him, "God is going to strike you, you whitewashed wall! Are you sitting to judge me according to the law, and yet contrary to the law you order me to be struck?" Those who stood by said, "Would you revile God's high priest?" And Paul said, "I did not know, brothers, that he was the high priest, for it is written, 'You shall not speak evil of a ruler of your people.'"
Acts 23:1-5

And he came to the sheepfolds by the way, where there was a cave, and Saul went in to relieve himself. Now David and his men were sitting in the innermost parts of the cave. And the men of David said to him, "Here is the day of which the Lord said to you, 'Behold, I will give your enemy into your hand, and you shall do to him as it shall seem good to you.'" Then David arose and stealthily cut off a corner of Saul's robe. And afterward David's heart struck him, because he had cut off a corner of Saul's robe. He said to his men, "The Lord forbid that I should do this thing to my lord, the Lord's anointed, to put out my hand against him, seeing he is the Lord's anointed." So David persuaded his men with these words and did not permit them to attack Saul. And Saul rose up and left the cave and went on his way. 1 Samuel 24:3-7 (I encourage you to read all of 1 Samuel 24.)

Lord, Show Me How to Go Lower

Oh God, remove the domestication of spirit that has settled in my heart and flesh! Oh God please forgive me of my attitude toward others. I've been like the master who was forgiven much, walking around demanding payment from those who've taken from me, forgetting the enormous debt you wiped clean from my account. Please forgive me for seeking justice in the flesh instead of recognizing that their need for you and for your mercy is no more than mine. Lord, I don't want to stay here; I can't stay here. Move me from this place and shake my soul. Show me how to go lower! I want to go lower! I can't understand how or why you have shown me such love, grace and mercy...yet, I find it in my heart to not reciprocate that to my fellow man? As if I'm better than they are? Uh! I'm wretched. I shake my head at others who are struggling in bondage, wondering why they don't lay it down. God I'm so sorry! Please forgive me God! Help me to see them as you see them, to love them how you love them! I NEED YOU GOD! I'm dirty without you! I'm rotten without you! I'M LOST WITHOUT YOU! God I want to love others without condition. I want to love them purely. They are beautiful. They are yours! Please forgive me for turning people away from you through my pride and arrogance. Please send someone to show them your genuine love! Would you give me another chance Lord? I will go again. I will do whatever it takes to make peace. You are the only Way, the Truth, and the Life! God, fill me, touch me, cleanse me! I'm your servant! In Jesus' holy and mighty name, amen.

Matthew 18:21-25; John 13; Romans 15; Philippians 2 and 1 Peter 2

Tending to Our Salvation

Are we tending to our salvation and what we have heard or are we drifting away from it?

What does it look like to tend to our salvation?

Therefore we must PAY MUCH CLOSER ATTENTION to what we have HEARD (full Gospel), lest we DRIFT AWAY from it. For since the message declared by angels proved to be reliable, and every transgression or disobedience received a just retribution, HOW SHALL WE ESCAPE IF WE NEGLECT such a great SALVATION? It was declared at first by the Lord, and it was attested to us by those who heard, while God also bore witness by signs and wonders and various miracles and by gifts of the Holy Spirit distributed according to his will.

Hebrews 2:1-4

What does this look like in our lives? As I read and study scripture to get to know the heart of God I cannot help but be changed and transformed. I recall reading Romans 15 one morning in early January 2020. I could have easily finished that chapter in minutes; however, Holy Spirit penetrated my heart with two simple phrases that have wrecked me in a good way. When I read the part that says, "Jesus did not seek to please himself," and then "He became a servant," I was undone. I literally sat in that chair for hours, pondering, weeping, and asking.

I began to dialogue with the Lord, "Lord, how is it that THE KING of kings and LORD of lords stepped down from his royal throne and became a servant? Why would he do that? How could he do that? He did that for me, why Lord? And he didn't seek to please himself…I've searched scripture and I genuinely don't see anywhere that Jesus sought to please himself. Father, I desire to have a heart like this. How do I do it? How do I go lower? How do I become a servant? How do I seek not to please myself? Am I ready? Am I capable?"

This conversation went on for hours, then days and it still continues. It is still affecting me. Our church fasted for twenty-one days starting on January first. I was personally fasting every meal except the last, and at that, I was only taking in fruits and vegetables and certain meats. The children and I were watching a movie and I had a plate of carrots and strawberries. I only had two carrots left. Two of my daughters asked me if they could have a carrot. My spirit immediately bucked up and I spouted off, "These are my last two!" Now, we had a whole bag upstairs in the refrigerator, but I only had these last two on my plate. I was hungry. I had been looking forward to this meal all day. Then, Romans fifteen screamed at my spirit, "He didn't seek to please himself. He became a servant." Immediately I retracted my shameful response to my daughters and gave them my last two carrots.

I entered into a conversation with the Lord and repented. I asked him why was this greed still inside me. He kindly told me because I hadn't laid it down yet. It was then that I realized the control that food had over me. But it was also a wake-up call as to how selfish I truly was. I felt gross. I knew I couldn't tackle this one on my own and I had to seek the Lord's help. I had to pickup my cross daily until I became a giving person. I keep seeing the horrible images of Jesus being persecuted, mutilated beyond recognition, hanging on the cross alongside two criminals, and being scorned and beaten. Two carrots are nothing. Two carrots are embarrassing.

Lord, hep me cultivate my relationship with you and tend to my salvation. Help me to work out my salvation daily. I don't like what I'm seeing and I desire to be more like you. I love you Father. I thank you for revealing what's in my heart through the washing of your Word as I read. I thank you for showing me how to die and how to live through the perfect example of your Son, Jesus. Amen

Worthy of the Gospel

Oh Lord, let my manner of life be worthy of the Gospel of Christ. Help me see the areas where I haven't humbled myself. Help me see others through your eyes and heart. Father please help me lay my life down and genuinely seek the best for those around me. Please forgive me of the times I'm selfish, lazy, prideful, or harsh. Please be my energy and strength when I'm feeling weak and tired. Help me not grow weary of doing good. Lord, even today I've had thoughts that are not right, not reflecting your heart. I repent and receive your forgiveness. I ask you Holy Spirit, to flood my heart and soul with your truth, your love, your grace, your mercy...help my eyes to always be fixed on you Jesus. Lord, please help me be disciplined with the foods I eat and determined to exercise my body to keep up with the demands of ministry in my life. Please forgive me for ever thinking this body is mine. It is yours Lord, I give it all to you. Use me God. Send me Father.

I worship you and you alone God! You are my Savior, my Redeemer, my ever present help, my strong tower, my support, my strength, my light, my hope, my glory! In You I find rest, peace and joy! You are glorious in every way. You ride on the clouds in a chariot. You command the wind, rain, waves, stars, sun, moon and planets. You are Love! You are Life! You've raised me from ashes to life! You are the Great I Am! Glory to God! Hallelujah!!! King Jesus!
Amen!

Psalms; John 15:13; 1 Corinthians; Galatians 6; Ephesians 4 and Philippians 1:27

2 Timothy 2

No soldier gets *entangled in civilian pursuits* since *his aim* is to
please the one who enlisted him." (Verse 4)

(Our aim is to please God and not get distracted by civilian pursuits or desires.
Our focus should constantly be eternal.)

"Remind them…*not to quarrel about words*,
which *does no good*, but only *ruins the hearers.*" (Verse 14)

"*Avoid irreverent babble*, for *it will lead people* into more and more *ungodliness*…
upsetting the faith of some…" (Verse 16-18)

"Have *nothing* to do with *foolish, ignorant controversies*; you *know* that they *breed quarrels*.
And the *Lord's servant must not be quarrelsome* but *kind to everyone*,
able to teach, *patiently enduring evil*, correcting his opponents with *gentleness*…
that they may come to their senses and escape from the snare of the devil…." (Verse 23-26)

Lord, I pray that you help us to focus on the eternal things, the kingdom things. Help us seek to please you and you alone. Help our words not be quarrelsome and help us avoid irreverent babble. We do not want to upset the faith of others or lead others into ungodliness. We ask you to help us discern the ignorant controversies and to avoid them, having nothing to do with them. We want no part of quarrels. Lord, we look to your example of your Son, Jesus to know how to be kind to everyone, being able to teach and patiently endure the evil of those know no better. Help us to correct the lost with gentleness, love, honor and grace that they may escape the snares of the enemy and turn to you oh Lord. Thank you for leading us and teaching us how to be dedicated to your kingdom work and not getting distracted by worldly things. We exalt you Lord and submit our hearts to your Lordship. Amen.

We are still looking for a political and military king and completely missing THE KING.

The Train of His Robe Filled the Temple

The Lord is AWESOME!

I've been in a time of worship this evening.

WOW!

As I was pouring out my praise and worship to my King, a song about the train of his robe filling the temple played. I pictured Messiah's **white** robe, long and magnificent.

Then the words from Isaiah 6:5-8 were sung that talks about being a man of unclean lips and the seraphim cleansing his lips with hot coals right before he dies. Its a beautiful scripture.
Then he gave me a picture of me surrendering to him and his authority and as I did this he touched my tongue with coal and then his **white** (Purity) robe **filled** the temple (My body, mind and spirit)!!! The robe symbolizes authority. His pure white robe of authority filled me, every part of me. Nothing else was left because his authority filled every space! He cleansed and purified me, every part of me!!!

I needed to receive this revelation today because I've felt convicted of so many areas of my heart! I felt I have failed my Lord and others miserably because of the pride, arrogance and offense that I was experiencing in my heart. But this revelation brings me such joy and peace and rest! Glory to God!! HALLELUJAH!!!

Maybe you need to hear this too. I pray it encourages you!
Let Holy Spirit speak to your heart! Be blessed in Jesus' name!

Isaiah 6

Maranatha! Come Lord Jesus!

The Lord is totally calling people together and uniting our hearts with his! More and more people are seeing what the Lord is doing and about to do.

I call my friends to submit wholly to the King of Kings! Lay down every other god or idol in your life and surrender to the Lord God! He's calling forth the messengers and watchmen and bringing in the nations under his Constitution!

I'm seeing people lay down religion and legalism. I'm seeing people's eyes open to the urgency of the hour!

This phrase is remarkably insightful—"You cannot, in truth, ask God to bless your reliance on anyone other than God." Tom Stolz *End-Time Babylon*

Think about it, asking God to bless our government and political system to preserve our "freedom" and rights? Who is it that has the authority and power to grant these things other than the Lord of Hosts, God Almighty?!

Lord, help us see that the only way we'll survive is not if America, or any other nations does. The only way we'll survive in the eternal realm is by laying our life down and **kneeling** before the cross, repenting, and surrendering to King Jehovah!

Matthew 25 and Revelation

Eternal Gospel

04FEB2021

The Bible is the only Book and real-life drama that has no end. If we're not including the return of Jesus and his eternal reign in our daily spiritual walk and discipleship we're abandoning the core message of the Eternal Gospel. When we accept Jesus as Lord we're not merely saved from hell; we are saved from sin and invited into eternal relationship with God at that begins the moment of our spiritual death to self and resurrection into Christ. Salvation is for today, right now, not just at our physical death.

We need to be talking about the returning Messiah, The Last Days, and his eternal reign because we are included in all three. The way we live now will determine how and where we will live eternally. If we are putting off the result of our salvation until physical death we may find that we are not allowed into the Marriage Supper of The Lamb. Jesus' blood paid for us to enter into our salvation today!

Understanding this, how should we then live?

#MARANATHA!

Matthew 25; Luke 13; Revelation

Seasons

As I sit in our study, coffee in hand, fire burning, Bible open...I gaze at the peacefully falling snowflakes, each original in design. I giggle because weathermen did not forecast anymore snow since early yesterday morning, and yet, God has continually dropped trillions upon trillions of individual snowflakes from heaven since then.

Winter is beautiful, peaceful, snuggly...fun. Its frigid temperatures will test the inner fortitude of man as he goes about his workday. It brings families together around a campfire, cuddling close. It's a time of giving and caring. Snow sledding, skiing, and if you're brave, hiking. Lots of hot coffee. Large family gatherings and big-eyed kids ripping paper off their gifts. Hustle and bustle. Christmas decorations frantically going up, trying to outdo last year and your neighbors. Holiday music repeating in the stores. Who has the coolest snow pictures? Icicles, freezing temps, frozen pipes, black ice. Four-wheel drive is helpful. Bright berries pop against the

65

stark white snow flocking the evergreens. Red cardinals sing their song. Peaceful. Cozy. But winter also finalizes the death that fall began.

As it prepares for winter, fall delivers robust, gorgeous color, amazing, feel-good temperatures where windows are open. You can feel the brisk breezes carry the nostalgic aromas of cinnamon and spice through comfy homes. The season for gathering. Gathering harvests and gathering around tables. The season of preparation for the cold and death of nature that is to come. Colorful leaves begin dropping to cover the ground in a majestic blanket of many colors. Probably my favorite season of all, is fall.

Prior to fall we were greeted with bright blue, clear skies, strong heat from the enormous sun, warm to almost uncomfortable temperatures, green grass, turning brown in some regions due to intense heat. You can hear laughter outdoors, lawn mowers, motorbikes, fireworks. It's a season of fun, joy, playing, hiking, sunbathing and swimming. Oceans are teeming with swimmers and children trying to escape the wave. Fishermen seeking to break records with the next big fish. World travels. Backyard barbecues. Family reunions. But before all this could happen it had to spring forth from budding seeds and warming temperatures. Spring.

Spring is another of my favorite seasons. Another opportunity for open windows, fresh, crisp breezes, ripe green leaves budding out, blooms bursting forth, the sun turning up the heat. You might see people standing or sitting, soaking in the warm and vitamin D that we so missed the previous cold season. Tops off Jeeps, sunroofs open, windows down, kayaks and canoes strapped, boats hauling behind. The water's still a little chilly, but who cares? The sun is out! "Spring showers bring May flowers!" And, possibly horrific tornadoes, torrential downfalls and flooding. "Turn around, don't drown!" But those flowers! How delightful they are! The aroma of spring! Easter dresses, Resurrection Sunday, family gatherings, photo ops, and what on earth do bunnies have to do with chicken eggs? Don't forget the spring cleaning, Pine Sol, almond oil on the wood, screens and windows cleaned. Everything's coming to life! Babies are being born.

As I sit here sipping my coffee on this 12°, snowy morning in front of my warm fire with my Bible Abba takes me through his perfection of creation. Who could have the wisdom to design a world such as this? Knowing that things would need to die in order to come to life and reproduce? Who could have known how to bring beauty with ashes? Who could have the power to position the earth to accommodate the circle of life so perfectly? And who could be such a majestic God and author of beauty that he knew exactly how to tell the story of the Gospel through creation, nature, the circle of life and the four seasons? But God…

1 Corinthians 15:35-49; John 12:24; Galatians 5:24; Romans 6:8 and Philippians 1:21

Prayer for You

I pray that you may be filled with knowledge of his will in all wisdom and spiritual understanding; that you may walk worthy of the Lord, fully pleasing him, being fruitful in every good work and increasing in the knowledge of God; strengthened with all might, according to his glorious power, for all patience and long suffering with joy; giving thanks to the Father who has qualified you to be a partaker of the inheritance of the saints in the light. He has delivered you from the power of darkness and conveyed you into the kingdom of the Son of his LOVE, in whom you have redemption, through his blood, the forgiveness of sins. He has reconciled you in the body of his flesh, through his death, to present you holy, and blameless, and above reproach in his sight! Continue in the faith, grounded and steadfast, not moved away from the hope of the Gospel. I pray that you know the riches of the glory of this mystery: which is Christ in you, the hope of glory!

You are seated in heavenly places!
You are a royal diadem and the apple of his eye!
You are a holy temple, a spiritual powerhouse!
You are a child of THE KING! YOU are LOVED...by THE KING!!!

Dreams and Thoughts from the Lord

Not Time to Celebrate

02FEB2017

In reading Numbers Nine and Ten this morning the Lord showed me something provocative and hopeful, and somewhat of a warning. Many in our nation have been celebrating the inauguration of President Trump, almost like a celebration of victory and conclusion. My dear brothers and sisters, as I've stated before, we must earnestly continue in steadfast prayer for our government, leaders, nation and the Church. We must also repent of the evil that we have allowed to take place in our nation. It has only been a couple of weeks since his inauguration and we have much work to do.

God showed me today that we must celebrate at the appointed time and not one minute before. We are not to celebrate prior to his appointed time and he will make that time known to us. We are to be cleansed as a nation before celebrating. That means we are to repent as a nation for the wicked we have done and have allowed to take place and we are to go in a new direction, his direction. We must never forget what he has brought us out of. At the Lord's command we are to move At the Lord's command we are to stay. At the Lord's appointed time we are to celebrate, but only after we have become cleansed and only when he says it's time.

Numbers 9-10 and 2 Chronicles 7

Protecting His Story

12JUL2017

I had a most intriguing dream where I was with my family and a few others (strangers) exploring a creek and areas on the bank. We saw a large stone-like monument or some type of artifact sculpture. The stone was sturdy. On this stone was a historical timeline story put together by individually carved stone tiles. They appeared to be in chronological order with the first being a tile of the baby Christ in a manger with a star above his head. The second was in Hebrew and dated the death of Christ. Somehow I knew what it said. The tile read, "Jehovah 30AD." There were many other stones in Hebrew and other languages that I couldn't read but knew them to be historical and chronological. I was able to push these tiles easily out of their positions and hold them in my hand, yet, no one else could get them out. Everyone wanted to handle them but for some reason I was guarding them, knowing they were fragile artifacts, yet the stone itself, was well built.

As I continued looking at the pieces in order I began seeing modern day timeline pieces and events such as Adolph Hitler, President Ronald Reagan, TV shows and human icons like professional athletes and Hollywood actors. I recognized Dora the Explorer and saw some TV show tile for the 1990s that I can't recall, yet I knew these tiles represented moral decay in our society. These tiles were hard and clear. Then, I came to the most intriguing tile of all. It was a circular type medallion with the drooping head of the persecuted Christ on the cross with blood-muddled hair draping his face and a thorn wreath penetrating his skull with blood dripping down. As I gently held it I vividly recall a young man's voice over my shoulder proclaiming, "Oh, that one is cool!" I remember feeling physically sorrowful and hurt by his remarks as I stared at my King's pain…the stone medallion began to crumble around the edges and I was desperate to protect it and keep it intact. I knew that as the medallion crumbled it signified a crumbling of real life, of society.

I was searching my spirit for how to prevent this crumbling. I gently and reverently replaced the tile in its place on the larger stone structure and began sharing with the children and young people who were showing up about each tile and their significance from beginning to end. I showed them the medallion of Christ and how the edges were beginning to crumble because it wasn't being cared for and explained that it is our duty to protect his story and keep it alive. Then, I woke-up…pondering that dream since yesterday. It was detailed and so surreal. I didn't want it to end. I wanted to learn more.

Two years later, on 08AUG2019 I had another dream in conjunction with the one above. There wasn't really any action to the dream other than another circular white stone medallion. On one side was a simple rectangular mark that I couldn't really make out. On the flip side was an image of a large ox head with horns. On the top left was a symbol that looked like a clock with one single hand that pointed to the one o'clock position. At the lower right corner was, "04m."

After conversing with our pastoral team here are some thoughts:

An ox represents a servant and humility but also great power (the large horns and strength), as does Jesus. Romans 15 tells us that he became a servant. Jesus' public ministry began around 30AD. This dream sounds like a call to proclaim Jesus to the next generation. The white stone medallion could represent purity. The 4m could represent 4,000 years as the lower case "m" in Greek means a thousand. The clock pointing to the one could indicate Jesus' first coming at around 4,000 years in the history of man.

Image of Jesus

DEC2017

In the dream I was sleeping but woke-up. I raised my head off the white linen pillow to look around (I was a little disoriented). Out of the corner of my eye I saw a shadow or markings appearing on my pillow. I looked closer and an image was appearing in a red clay color. It was a distinct image of Christ with a crown of thorns, blood masked, dark wavy hair with one tear drop under his left eye. I felt someone walking up behind me, then I saw the image lifting from the pillow.

A revelation came as I was watching *A.D.* Where the blood stains appeared on the linens of Jesus' burial clothes after his resurrection, a revelation of the promise of his coming; but this was a promise of his second coming. The tear drop symbolized his grief over a fallen world.

I also received a revelation that Jesus' image was fading, indicating that I was drawing back in sharing my faith around certain people because I didn't want to offend them or have them criticize my faith. The Lord made me realize I need not shrink back from faith for any reason. I was encouraged to begin expressing my full faith around this person and it has opened doors. Hallelujah!

It's King Jesus!

01APR2020 (Global Pandemic-COVID19)

I had a dream about the end last night!

I was sitting outside at a picnic table with one of my children and a friend and one of her daughters. We were at a park in the afternoon. It seemed like maybe an event was going on, like a concert or some kind of gathering. It was bright outside with the sun shining but there were clouds moving in.

As my friend was about to leave I noticed these gold, dust particles falling from the sky. They were like solid chunks but then they would break apart, as if they were disintegrating, but they would sort of sizzle before reaching the ground. The sky was becoming darker but the gold specks glittered. You could see everyone starting to notice them and wondering what it was. As the gold dust sparkled and fell, to the left a magnificent, bright light appeared in the sky. It was getting closer. It became so bright and magnificent that not only could we not look at it but our bodies naturally started falling to the ground because the brightness was so overwhelming and intruding.

I began yelling, "Jesus! It's Jesus! King Jesus! Holy, holy, holy, Jesus Come Lord, come!" I thought about all my children...where are they? An absolute peace rushed over me and a voice in my spirit made it known that they were also witnessing this and we would all be together shortly.

The next scene....we were inside a huge market area. We were there together as families, standing in a loose line of sorts and a man, just a regular looking man began speaking, *"You will begin to see things take place that you used to be against. Things that you rejected and fought against, but now you will begin to accept them and submit to them. Everyone will be fed, everyone will be taken care of. No one will have less than anyone else and no one will have more than anyone else. You will all have access to the same things and the same amount."*

That guy started disappearing and another man started to transposed in his place. This man started right where the other man left off and continued saying similar things, *"You are all counted and covered. No one is higher than the other or more significant. Money no longer matters."* This man was Jesus. He was glorious! Family groups began moving toward him and everyone was calmly lining up without chaos, panic, or selfishness; everyone tamely moved toward Jesus. Then I woke-up.

Time of Acceleration

19JUN2020

I had an intriguing dream last night set in the present day. I was mostly watching the scene, not in it and I'm not sure if I can properly describe it. I was sitting somewhere but didn't recognize it. I was looking down on the scenes unfolding on the earth, mostly America, with all the hate, dissension, racism, riots, vandalism, killing, etc. It was as if I was in my earthly father's room (that comfortable), my father being the Lord. He wasn't sitting next to me in the physical, but it felt like he was sitting next to me. I never really saw a form but I knew he was there. It's difficult to explain. But we were "sitting" next to each other.

I was sad to see everything taking place on the earth and tears began to drip from my face. Then, I heard him say, *"This is a time of acceleration."* I knew he was referring to the *things taking place* and they were going to *increase in frequency and escalate in severity*. This caused me to feel a little overwhelmed.

Knowing my loved ones and many friends were still down there I began pleading on their behalf and *praying* for strength and wisdom. My Father said to me again, *"This is a time of acceleration."* Now I knew he was speaking of prayer. He was telling me it was time to accelerate, to increase in frequency and intensity, our prayers for the people of the earth.

I saw people I didn't know but had such a love for them as if I knew them personally, like family. They were people who many might not consider family if they really were family. There were lots of young people, young adults. Many of the men looked like women and many women looked like men. There were lots of colors of hair, piercings, tattoos, and clothing that revealed private body parts. It was a party type scene where they were involved in sexual-type activity. There were people openly using drugs and drinking massive amounts of alcohol. It was a scene of disorder. I felt such a love for them that I could feel this uneasy knot in my gut. More tears streamed from my eyes. I felt as if I was looking at a loved one that was about to die and I wanted to urgently tell them something but wasn't sure they could hear me. My Father spoke a third time, *"This is a time of acceleration."* This time, He was speaking of *love*. He was trying to get me to see how important it is to accelerate our love for the lost and to show them compassion and treat them with dignity.

The next scene I was in a big room with several others. Maybe twenty to thirty. Several I recognized, but most I didn't. I did, however, know that we were like family, working together toward the same thing. We were praying. We were praying intensely for all the things above and it was very loud, but not unorganized or disorderly. I could feel a sense of authority and calmness as we prayed, not panic or fear.

This is a time of ACCELERATION.

The scene ended.

Last Hours

13JUL2018

I worked as a part-time hospice companion sitter. This is an account from one of those sittings. I sat with an eminent patient, "JP," at the nursing home on Thursday 12JUL2018. JP was in pain. His ex-wife and son live two minutes away and hadn't been to see him in years. I prayed that they would show up for some possible reconciliation. Several hours later they arrived. It was not a great visit and he was physically distressed while they were present. I prayed that his passing would be quick and peaceful. I prayed over him and interceded for him for forgiveness for the first several hours. He seemed to wince every time I'd say, "Jesus," but I pushed on. By the end of my shift I could say Jesus' name and he was more relaxed and peaceful. The next sitter arrived at 6:00pm so I said my good-byes to JP, wondering if I'd see him the next day. The next morning (after my husband left for work, so after 5:30am), I had a lucid dream that the sitter called to tell me he had just passed away. I asked if his family made it back up before he passed. I remember saying he was free from pain now. I woke up around 6:00am and had my Bible and prayer time and then called the office at 9:00am to give my hours for the previous day. I asked how the patient was and the administrator said he passed at 7:20am. I believe he received Jesus before his passing and this dream was Abba's way of showing me that.

02SEP2020

I dreamed the gas company team was at our house searching for a leak on the first floor of our home near our son's room. A lady thought she found it and she was new. She lit a lighter to see if the flame would flare. It did, big. A supervisor ran over and choked the flame out with a metal cap on the furnace and walked away. But the flame reignited and began spreading quickly. I yelled, "Fire! Kids get out!" The children ran out to the street. I ran back for my Bible and family pictures. As we stood at the street we witnessed flames filling the attic.

In the realm of reality I woke-up the next morning and walked around the perimeter of our home. When I came upon the gas meter I could smell gas. I immediately called the gas company and told them about my dream and the fact that I smelled gas. I requested someone right away. They were there within minutes. We had a gas leak. The gas company repaired it.

I believe this was also a prophetic message to Believers (to me) to caution fellow Believers to realign with God's heart. That activities are coming that are going to catapult the days of tribulation.

Those who are lukewarm or wayward need our help.

The Book of Revelation

Scroll Unrolling

16SEP2020

Last night's dream was extremely sobering. I was among mostly strangers while out running errands as the sky began darkening. It was obvious something was happening. Many suspected a tornado. But the darkness was intensifying and I knew it was more than a tornado. This was weather system was more beyond natural. Winds were picking up tremendously. As we were watching the horizon the most bizarre thing happened. It was as if the horizon was on a long, horizontal movie screen, or a scroll. Its size was enormous. As we gazed at the horizon we saw the scroll rolling to the right, running through various weather patterns. It would get violent and stormy, then sunny and bright. It would become overcast and snowy and then leaves would begin turning colors and it would get breezy. This occurred in a matter of minutes. Then....the movie screen horizon began picking up tremendous speed. It was quite alarming! The weather patterns were running through the seasons immensely fast. We were experiencing trembles on the earth, hail, there was a great deal of lightning.

People began panicking. I knew what was happening and I started yelling as loudly as I could, "REPENT! REPENT! REPENT! Hurry, we're running out of time! REPENT! Don't delay! Don't be afraid, just repent!"

I began running through the town and trying to warn people to repent and accept Jesus. Some did, but many did not. What was most alarming was that there were people I knew and loved who rejected the opportunity with great pride and indignation. Even more alarming, there were some who had previously said they were Christians but weren't. Some of them even taught in church or led classes or prayer groups. I remember physically feeling sorrow for them. It was sobering. The sorrow and grief over these arrogantly rejecting

Jesus, especially those whom society knew as powerful Christians, was almost too heavy for me. But I couldn't spend time there, I had to move on and keep warning others because so many were still panicking and in shock, not understanding what was happening. The last scene I remember was someone very special to me who boasted that they would not repent because they didn't need to. They rejected the idea that Jesus was real, even after seeing and experiencing this most bizarre weather/geological event rapidly unfolding.

I woke-up, grieved and alarmed.

Please, if you haven't repented of your sins and accepted Jesus as your ONLY Lord and Savior, please don't delay, do it right now. If you have questions I'm willing to do my best to answer them and what I can't answer we'll find the answers.

Heaven and hell are real. Jesus is real. God is real. God is the Creator of all things. His only Son, Jesus, suffered, died on the cross, bore our sins, was resurrected and is alive today. He sits at the right of the Father and is returning for his people. Not everyone will go with him to the final heaven or be with him for the thousand-year reign on earth. In fact, the Bible tells us few will enter, but many will choose the path that leads to destruction.

You can't do anything to earn salvation except repent of your sins and accept the free gift of grace and mercy that is the Lord Jesus Christ. You have to submit to his authority in your life in every area. You cannot serve two masters. You must die to self and be raised new with Jesus as a new creation.

Please, don't delay.

Grace and Peace Multiplied

18SEP2020

"May GRACE and PEACE be MULTIPLIED to you IN the KNOWLEDGE of GOD and of JESUS our LORD."

2 Peter 1:2 ESV

Grace and peace are attainable but only as our personal knowledge of God occurs. Just knowing about God won't bring much grace and peace. Knowing the man Jesus and his devotion to the Father and love for us; knowing the Father and his gentle, merciful, loving and patient ways; and knowing Holy Spirit in intimacy, recognizing his voice and presence and power births the revelation of grace and peace as his heart causes our heart to be transformed and aligned with his.

As we see how gracious and slow to anger Father is with us, we become more gracious and slow to anger with others.

As we witness the servant heart, humility and selfless love of Jesus we can't help but go lower in humility and seek not to please ourselves but to genuinely be concerned for the needs of those around us.

As we experience the manifestations of Holy Spirit through his speaking, power, glory and many ways of interacting we begin to realize how truly meek we are and that we need Holy Spirit to receive a clear and genuine revelation of God through his Son by Holy Spirit! He reveals the glory of the Son Jesus to us and when we see Jesus, we have seen the Father!

We experience Holy Spirit as he speaks words of confirmation, knowledge and wisdom through the voice of those around us. He points our hearts to the awesome acts of creation that exist in the solar system, circle of life, and geological constructs of this planet and all of its weather systems and the inspiring creation of all life that is present to us, such as the singing cardinal who cares for its young with the food provided by Creator. We see him and his glory in the way a ewe births her lamb and nurses it to independence, or how a human conceives, carries the baby in utero and then births the baby and nurses it to its next stage of independence only to repeat the circle of life.

We experience Holy Spirit in dreams, music, prayer and worship. We taste the promises of grace and Holy Spirit reminds us of God's promises and truths which brings peace through the knowledge of Abba's grace.

Hallelujah!!!

Glory to God!

06OCT2020

I often feel inadequate intellectually, incapable of delivering my thoughts in an articulate way in which the hearer can understand (One of many reasons I often share straight scripture, besides it speaks for itself). Often I don't feel knowledgeable enough to share scripture. I know what I believe and that when I read God's Word I can't walk away unchanged. I do have some questions shelved until I see Jesus face to face. I carry a burden and great respect for the living Word of God, recognizing the power it carries. I may get some things wrong here and there but what I can promise you is that my heart is burdened for others to know Truth, to know The Living One, on a very deep and personal level. I can tell you I don't know it all nor will I ever claim to. But what I do know is HIM! And that's my heart's desire for you: to know the Lord personally. I desire to encourage others to seek him and to know him, that you dwell in his presence and be transformed and made new by the washing of his Word and by the power of his testimony.

Please don't ever take my word for it. I always encourage you to seek Truth yourself. (Truth is a man, Jesus.) I will always encourage you to search him out personally. Remember, Messiah, our Bridegroom is returning to judge the earth.

Come, Let us prepare!

MARANATHA!

Present Day

15OCT2020

Present day, United States of America.

First, I remember walking along war-ridden streets that looked like a scene from the Middle East. As I was walking I was on the phone with my husband as he gave me survival instructions. I recall asking him the fastest and most painless way to take my own life if it came to that. (I don't know if this is something I'd actually do. Who can say?)

There were multiple soldiers clearly on the same team, yet from different countries. China, North Korea, Russia, Colombia, and the US were teaming up. There was an emblem or patch that some folks had on their clothing while others of us didn't. The population was quite sparse at this point and many buildings and structures already destroyed, so hiding was challenging.

I managed to hide under a walking ramp to an apartment and while there I witnessed an Asian man who spoke English showing soldiers where a person lived. Once they found the person they let the Asian man go. The Asian man found me and hid with me under the ramp. We laid there for some time when the same group of soldiers came back by. It was cold and wet. They too, were Asian and didn't speak English well at all. They were searching for someone else now. We were laying extremely still and quiet. The soldiers were leaving, we thought. As they were walking away one soldier walked toward the ramp and had a dog on a leash sniff out the ramp. The dog exposed us and they all came running with flashlights. They pulled out the Asian guy and motioned me to come out as well. They put the person on their knees that the Asian man exposed and shot him in the forehead while the guy watched. Then they made us both get on our knees and gave me a golf ball. One soldier told me to toss it up in the air repeatedly while I said scripture out loud. I was whispering it because I was nervous and wasn't quite sure what they were wanting. He acted like he was friendly toward us but I didn't trust him. As I continued tossing the golf ball in the air I got louder and bolder reciting scripture and saying a prayer and declaring loudly, "Jesus, you're truth! Jesus, you're light! Jesus, you're truth! Jesus, you're light!" They raised their rifles aiming at my mouth...I woke-up.

There was quite a bit more, but I believe this is sufficient. It was so clear. So many people were in great panic. Others calm and strong. Many were extremely confused, while others were carelessly complacent and ignorantly defiant, as if nothing was happening. They were going about their workday, but then would suffer for it in horrendous ways. It was very surreal.

There was definitely a shortage of food because I saw several people searching dumpsters and bartering with others for food and coats (I believe it was winter).

Will the Modern Day Church Survive the End-Times?

25OCT2020

As I'm trying to fall asleep to wake-up only a few hours from now I'm thinking about how God has been speaking to the American Church and attempting to grab our attention to gain a revelation of the Acts 2:42 Church. As the normal ways of church have been tested, interrupted and altered are we listening to the Father and seeking his voice on how to move forward in how we do church, or are we attempting to resurrect an old way that perhaps he is calling us to leave behind? Perhaps it was never his way to begin with.

The Church has attempted to prolong the life of the modern American Church that has been propped up by materialistic prosperity, gadgets, entertainment and events with strictly rehearsed man-made schedules and agendas.

Perhaps God is trying to speak to us and call us into the way he wants us to do church.

What will happen when the next major economic crisis hits America? And it will. These last few were just speed bumps preceding what's to come. The modern American Church will not survive the upcoming big crash. We must seek the Lord's voice and gain revelation for how he wants us doing church. We can gain a lot of insight from our brothers and sisters in the Middle East, Africa, and Asia.

Will we be able to stand for a church service with no sound equipment, no children's Sunday School or youth group? Will we be okay sitting around in a circle reading straight from the scrolls? Will we be able to endure hours of prayer without a worship team on a stage with fog machines? Will we be OK with meeting in someone's small house for church and communion? Will the pastors be able to survive without a pastor's salary? Will we be able to not be offended by these questions?
Or will we immediately jump up to defend why all these things are perfectly acceptable…even expected? Will we recognize that church is not the Savior of the nations but Jesus is?

Lord, open our ears, eyes and heart to what you are trying to tell us. Help us desire your model of Church. Please, soften our hearts to yours. In Jesus' name, amen.

Global Shift

24OCT2020

A major shift is occurring in our global society and culture, but mostly in the West. A lot of Christians are becoming more openly offended by the true, radical Gospel of Jesus Christ. There's a determination to not recognize Kingdom Culture as the standard, rather clinging to a retarded gospel that is centered around "self."

Simultaneously, I'm seeing an increase in those who've tried "Church" and have been hurt or disappointed, causing them to return to searching and walking in the reality and pursuit of the true definition of Christianity. This group wasn't convinced by religious shows, traditions or activities but are encountering a spiritual revelation of what Kingdom of Heaven culture looks like. In fact, this group of people is seeing and understanding with almost more purity and truth that following Jesus costs something...no, it costs everything, and they are willing to pay that cost. Today, this cost often looks like standing out from a people who are worshiping something altogether different. They are being ridiculed, chastised and ostracized for their beliefs, very different way of thinking and especially…how they love. The world and even parts of the Church are don't understand how or why they are loving the most unlovable and undeserving. They don't comprehend why they see things so differently and it greatly offends them. The more this group increases and the louder they become by displaying the heart of the Father the more offended and outraged the other "religious" group becomes.

The other group is clinging to, fighting for and demanding their way that is fueled by a worldly way of thinking. The first group is giving up more self and serving the least of these among society. They are giving up their personal time and foregoing higher incomes and pleasures to spend time in the House of Prayer with fellow Jesus Freaks.

A great divide is beginning. Many will continue to be outraged by the culture of heaven being displayed as it clashes with every ideal they've clung to. They will insist that their way is right and that things must be done their way otherwise everything will fall apart.

The first group will press on, unoffended by the dogmatic screams and shouts, realizing that the storm is coming and time is short. They are preparing for the storm that has been promised and prophesied while the other group is fighting to preserve and maintain something that was promised and prophesied to be utterly destroyed.

"And if it is evil in your eyes to serve the Lord, choose this day whom you will serve, whether the gods your fathers served in the region beyond the River, or the gods of the Amorites in whose land you dwell. But as for me and my house, we will serve the Lord."

Joshua 24:15

Acknowledgements

I would like to thank some very special people who have inspired and encouraged me in this project. They are probably not even aware of how much they have impacted me. In no particular order:

Jennifer Smallwood has the biggest heart I've ever encountered. Her attitude and thought process is much like mine, kindred spirits indeed. She has shown me how to truly hear from the Holy Spirit and always ask him before I make a decision. She has helped me discover there is much less black and white and way more gray than I was comfortable with; but through our friendship she has shown me how to embrace the gray through the heart of the Father. She is my go-to person when I need to talk things out. Jennifer is so full of grace, mercy, honor, and refining truth. She speaks my language and knows how to encourage me. She was the first person to point me to Jesus in the most intimate and personal way, showing me that relationship with him was truly accessible and necessary. I am incredibly thankful for my dear sister and love her with all my heart. (<u>You are Worthy Ministries</u>)

Corey Russell has a beautiful heart for the Lord and it overflows with deep, genuine desire to know Jesus more. He has also pointed me to the intimate friendship of Jesus. I first met Corey at an intense breakout session at One Thing in Kansas City, MO, put on by International House of Prayer. I knew immediately that he was a man after God's heart. Corey has such a gentle, yet bold character. He started Zoom Bible Studies during the global pandemic in 2020. We would meet four to five days a week digging deeply into the scriptures. This family of believers was a hiding place of encouragement and fountain of fresh water for me this past year.

He is humble, patient and hungry to know Jesus more. Corey never makes any course about himself but always points to Christ. He genuinely desires to lead others into deeper intimacy with the Lord. It was through these courses that I began to yearn for a deeper intensity in knowing God and his character. I am extremely grateful for Corey and his passion and child-like excitement for Jesus. (www.coreyrussellonline.com)

Candace Kirkpatrick was kind enough to read my manuscript and share her thoughts and give me feedback in such loving and gentle ways. She is full of love, life, and joy. We knew we had a sisterly connection as we watched one another share our hearts for the Lord on Facebook. I am so grateful the Lord introduced us. She called me after reading the first half of my manuscript and as she shared her heart with me about the emotions Holy Spirit drew out in her as she read *Captivated*, I literally wept because everything she said was exactly what I prayed this book would deliver. She has encouraged me to draw out the love of the Father through his Word and gentle character. I deeply value our friendship and her genuine heart for the Lord.

The Bride of Christ Family has been meeting via Zoom since March of 2020. Our family has grown since, of faithful saints who patiently await the return of our Bridegroom, Jesus, the Messiah. This family sharpens like iron and motivates and encourages in ways the Church desperately needs in this hour. To you, my family, I love you dearly and am forever grateful for each of you! Maranatha!

Reviews of Captivated

Reading Ann's book brought me into the Presence of the Lord in a beautiful intimate way. I felt as Mary must have felt sitting at the feet of Jesus, taking in every word of the Master. Every other voice is silenced when we hear Him. Reading each page brought a greater intimacy, a greater hunger for more of God in my life. There was such a tenderness, a gentleness that allowed me to become more vulnerable before Jesus. Knowing He waits with loving, open arms intensifies my desire for Him and He never disappoints. Ann portrays Jesus in His glory while revealing His desire for our love in return. Thank you, Ann, for baring your heart and showing us how we can come closer to Jesus. I absolutely love it. I feel the Presence of the Lord reading it. At times I feel I'm treading on holy ground. I love the illustrations. I definitely believe the Holy Spirit overshadows this writing. Ann has written with such depth of intimacy while delivering it in understandable language. Every page points to Jesus, causing a longing for more of Him. I had to stop and savor every passage as Jesus was revealed. He truly is Captivating! —Marsha Frederick Hayes

Ann's book is beautifully written. It is inspiring, encouraging, and challenging. She has packed this book full of powerful messages of God's love. The words, quotes, and pictures will draw you closer to the one who loves you most. This is a treasure to cherish. Don't rush through it, take your time, and enjoy. —Lena Lamore

"Very uplifting and intimate read. You can feel the authenticity of a heart that has been transformed by the King of Glory. From a young girl's encounter through the journey into adulthood each word draws you in and encapsulates this beautiful relationship between Abba and His precious child. Author Ann Lindholm expresses a sincere sentiment and conveys a message of returning back to your first love thus cultivating a deep intimate relationship with the one who first loved us. Definitely take your time while soaking in the beauty found within these pages and allow yourself to be *Captivated* by Jesus." —Danay Vela

Titles by Ann Lindholm

Love to Reconcile: The Heart of the Father

(Also available in Español)

Love to Reconcile focuses on healing and reconciliation with the Lord and with others through the act of forgiveness. Practical tools are shared as well as the heart of the Father, which is that all people would be reconciled to Him and with one another.

You can purchase *Love to Reconcile* in paperback or digital format:

www.hispublishinghouse.com

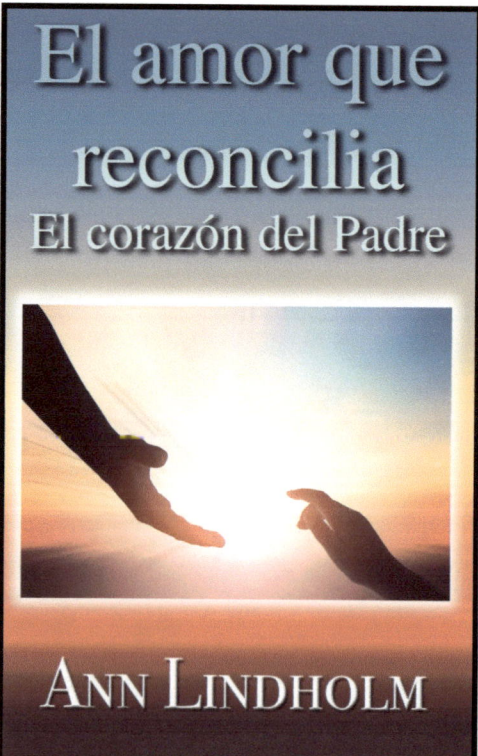

Reviews of *Love to Reconcile*

Jane Saladino-Yoas: Beautifully and lovingly written! Ann reminds us that no sin is bigger than God, and that He loves us no matter what sin we have committed. Ann uses her knowledge and understanding of the Bible to bring us many examples of God's love and forgiveness for us when we repent of our sins. I would recommend this book for anyone who is in need of reconciliation, and who among us isn't?

Brett Crisp: I bought your e-book this morning. I couldn't stop reading. I finished it before I had to go to work. Two words...Absolute Truth!

Jacqueline Bills: The author, Ann Lindholm, did an excellent job revealing the Father's heart from Old Testament all the way through the New Testament with His desire for reconciliation with His children. Using scripture and personal revelation, she brings to light His great love and desire for relationship with every individual. She goes on to share not only His desire for individuals to be in right relationship with Him, but also His desire for our relationships with each other to be reconciled to love and peace and even our nation to be reconciled to God. Ann uses many relevant scriptures to highlight His heart and finishes the book with thought provoking tools to use for application of the reader. Every person, whether far off from God or actively seeking the Lord, will benefit from this book.

Reviews of *Love to Reconcile* continued

Holley Watts - This is a beautifully written book about how God's love for us is bigger than we realize sometimes. Ann uses her knowledge of the Word coupled with personal testimony to remind the reader we are never too far from God, despite what we may think. I love that this book is full of specific scripture references, it makes it so easy to follow along and have a bible study at the same time! The helpful tools at the end are amazing as well! Way to go Ann!

Amazon Customer -Beautifully and lovingly written! Ann reminds us that no sin is bigger than God, and that He loves us no matter what sin we have committed. Ann uses her knowledge and understanding of the bible to bring us many examples of God's love and forgiveness for us when we repent of our sins. I would recommend this book for anyone who is in need of reconciliation, and who among us isn't?"Just" a Housewife: Shaping Future Generations

"Just" a Housewife: The Powerful Role that Shapes Generations

The forgotten and often neglected role of housewife has led to a broken society. In "Just" a Housewife the author will explore why this important role must be resurrected to save future generations. From a biblical standpoint, "Just" a Housewife touches on every aspect of the role from homemaking to health, from childrearing to cooking. You won't want to miss the highly sought after recipes at the end either! Hear about amazing testimonies regarding her children's miraculous healing and protection in the Family Health chapter! Sit back, grab a cup, or a pot of coffee, and join her on the journey of being "Just" a Housewife.

You can purchase *"Just" a Housewife* in paperback or digital form at:
www.hispublishinghouse.com

Reviews of *"Just" a Housewife*

Barbara Y. -I could not put it down. It was so rich with God's Word and godly advice. She makes no bones about the the fact that there is nothing at all wrong with working moms, and every wife can certainly get something great out of this book. But this book is geared more towards the housewife (obviously). It was great to read a book by an author who "gets" what it is like to be a housewife/stay at home mom. I felt validated, and encouraged. I hope that many housewives, especially newlyweds, get ahold of this book as early as possible in their relationships, and pray it helps them to avoid some of the most common sources of marital strife.

Sara Atkinson -As a stay stay at home mom of ten years, I really enjoyed this book! Ann shares scripture,
insight, practical tips, recipes, and most importantly encouragement for women who are choosing to live counter culture and embrace Titus 2 living. Whether you are a seasoned SAHM or fresh out of the work force and trying to find your footing in your role at home, you will appreciate the wisdom and refreshment this book offers. And it's a quick and easy read, a bonus for this of us with young kiddos!!

Mario Guzman -I thoroughly enjoyed Ann's book, Just a Housewife! This is a very practical guide for those who have responded to the highest calling a woman can accept--- and that is one of a housewife or homemaker. Even though this book may offer some obvious solutions, for many in today's culture being a housewife has all but become a lost art. I love how the author describes the importance of being supportive, and recognizing who the head of the household truly is, God. I found her personal stories and somewhat of a Christian Dear Abbey approach to housekeeping inspiring and refreshing. She also includes some long time favored recipes which I am excited about trying out, as well. I know that if you are wondering about how to be a better housewife, mother and successful woman in the home, you will enjoy this read!

Amazon Customer -Ann Lindholm's book, "Just" a Housewife, highlights the often overlooked profession of homemaking and motherhood, and through Ann's sage wisdom and personal experience, equips women with the tools to create a loving environment where bonding can occur and the family develop deep, Christ centered relationships with one other. From practical examples to heartwarming memories, Ann outlines how a healthy home is essential to the family as well as society. An excellent read! Great as a gift or for personal enjoyment.

Rebecca Darga -Ann is very direct and to the point, she is very open and honest about real life. I personally loved her chapters on raising disciples and homeschooling.

Get updates for new releases and special events!

Sign up at:

www.hispublishinghouse.com

About the Author

Ann Lindholm is the wife of a former US Army Ranger, mother of four children, one son-in-law and Nona to a granddaughter. In addition to writing Ann home schools her three younger children, is a full-time homemaker, works part-time for My Father's World homeschool curriculum and builds websites. She is a devout follower of Jesus Christ and attempts to be led by the Spirit in all that she does. Although she has not arrived, she has learned a great deal through personal life experiences. Ann became an unwed mother at age nineteen. She has experienced some personal trauma in her life that she has had to overcome emotionally and spiritually. She raised her children for twelve years while her husband was deployed or away at training faithfully serving our great nation. She gave her life completely to Christ at the age of twenty-one. Her salvation experience was dramatic and life-changing as the Lord reached out to her while she was at her lowest. It is from these experiences and personal relationship and growth with the Lord that Ann passionately writes and yearns to share the love of Jesus with whomever will listen.

www.ingramcontent.com/pod-product-compliance
Lightning Source LLC
Chambersburg PA
CBHW041325290426

44109CB00004B/124